Cool STEAM Careers

Athletic Trainer

Samantha Bell

Published in the United States of America by Cherry Lake Publishing
Ann Arbor, Michigan
www.cherrylakepublishing.com

Content Adviser: Kevin Allen, NASM-Certified Personal Trainer
Reading Adviser: Marla Conn, ReadAbility, Inc.

Photo Credits: © Visionsi, cover, 1, 6; © Richard Ulreich/ZUMA Press/Newscom, 5; © kali9/iStock.com, 9; © vm/iStock.com, 10; © asiseeit/iStock.com, 12; © Walleyelj | Dreamstime.com - NFL - Pregame Stretching Photo, 15; © CEFutcher/iStock.com, 16 ; © Natursports/Shutterstock.com, 17; © Air Images/Shutterstock Images, 18; © Aspenphoto | Dreamstime.com - American Football Injury On The Field Photo, 21; © DNY59/iStock.com, 22; © aimintang/iStock.com, 25; © Monkey Business Images, 26; © ftwitty/iStock.com, 28

Copyright ©2016 by Cherry Lake Publishing
All rights reserved. No part of this book may be reproduced or utilized in
any form or by any means without written permission from the publisher.

Library of Congress Cataloging-in-Publication Data

Bell, Samantha.
 Athletic trainer/Samantha Bell.
    pages cm.—(Cool STEAM Careers)
 Includes index.
 ISBN 978-1-63362-555-6 (hardcover)—ISBN 978-1-63362-735-2 (pdf)—ISBN 978-1-63362-645-4 (paperback)—ISBN 978-1-63362-825-0 (ebook)
 1. Athletic trainers—Juvenile literature. I. Title.

 GV428.7.B45 2015
 796.092—dc23
                                2015005356

Cherry Lake Publishing would like to acknowledge the work of
the Partnership for 21st Century Skills. Please visit www.p21.org
for more information.

Printed in the United States of America
Corporate Graphics

ABOUT THE AUTHOR

Samantha Bell is a children's book writer, illustrator, teacher, and mom of four busy kids. Her articles, short stories, and poems have been published online and in print.

TABLE OF CONTENTS

CHAPTER 1
Watching Over Athletes 4

CHAPTER 2
Becoming an Athletic Trainer 8

CHAPTER 3
On the Job 14

CHAPTER 4
Benefits and Disadvantages 20

CHAPTER 5
Today and Tomorrow 24

THINK ABOUT IT 30
LEARN MORE 31
GLOSSARY 32
INDEX 32

STEAM is the acronym for Science, Technology, Engineering, Arts, and Mathematics. In this book, you will read about how each of these study areas is connected to a career in athletic training.

— CHAPTER 1 —

Watching Over Athletes

Jack cheered as his older sister, Jenny, scored again. Three minutes left in the basketball game! Suddenly, one of the players tripped. She fell down hard on her right knee on the gym floor.

The referee whistled, and the game stopped. The player was still on the floor, and she seemed to be in pain. Jack watched as the girl's coach and teammates rushed over to her. Someone else ran out on the court, too. He carried a first-aid kit. "Who's that?" Jack asked his mom.

"That's the visiting school's athletic trainer," Jack's

High school, college, and pro sports teams almost always have athletic trainers available on the sidelines.

mom replied. "He's going to see how badly the player is injured. Then he'll decide what needs to be done to help her."

When injuries occur during warm-ups, practice, games, or competitions, athletic trainers (ATs) are there to help their athletes. Sometimes the AT can treat the athlete's injuries. Other times, the injuries are more serious. Then the ATs get the athlete into a doctor's care immediately.

Treating injuries is only a small part of an athletic trainer's job. ATs also work hard to prevent injuries.

Some athletic trainers give athletes exercise to practice after injuries.

They set up exercise programs that help athletes warm up and stretch their muscles.

Some ATs work with high school sports teams, college teams, or professional teams. Others work for companies, hospitals, the military, or sports medicine clinics.

Athletic trainers have been working with athletes for more than 2,000 years. Some of the early trainers helped athletes prepare for the Olympic Games in ancient Greece. Later, in the Roman Empire, trainers worked with athletes who raced chariots pulled by teams of horses. In the mid-1800s, many people in the United States enjoyed taking part in sports. Some U.S. colleges started programs in gymnastics and football. At first, coaches and doctors took care of athletes' injuries. Then a few colleges started hiring special people to train, **condition**, and care for athletes. Those people were some of the first modern-day athletic trainers.

These early trainers did not have a degree or special training. They learned on the job and taught themselves the skills they needed. Today's ATs learn through college classes and hands-on experience. They are ready to prepare, care for, and rehabilitate our modern-day athletes.

THINK ABOUT ENGINEERING

Athletic trainers often have to think like engineers. Engineers look at a problem and figure out the best solution. When an athlete is injured, the athletic trainer must look at the injury and decide the best way to help. Sometimes the trainer can treat the athlete. Other times, the athlete will need to go to the hospital.

[COOL STEAM CAREERS]

— CHAPTER 2 —

Becoming an Athletic Trainer

Do you enjoy being physically active and playing sports? Are you interested in science and how the human body works? Do you like to help people? These are a few of the qualities athletic trainers should have. They also need good communication skills. They must be able to tell athletes how to take care of themselves. They have to let coaches know if an athlete is unable to play. They may have to explain an athlete's injury to a doctor.

Athletic trainers must be able to make good decisions quickly. When an injury occurs, they have to decide right

Chemistry classes can be helpful for future athletic trainers.

away on the best treatment. Having a strong stomach and a strong mind are important qualities, too. Sometimes athletic trainers must deal with blood and take care of broken bones. They also have to be firm with athletes, coaches, and parents who think athletes can play through their injuries.

Students can start preparing for this career in high school. They should take health and science classes such as biology and chemistry. Some high schools have the Athletic Training Student Aide Program where students

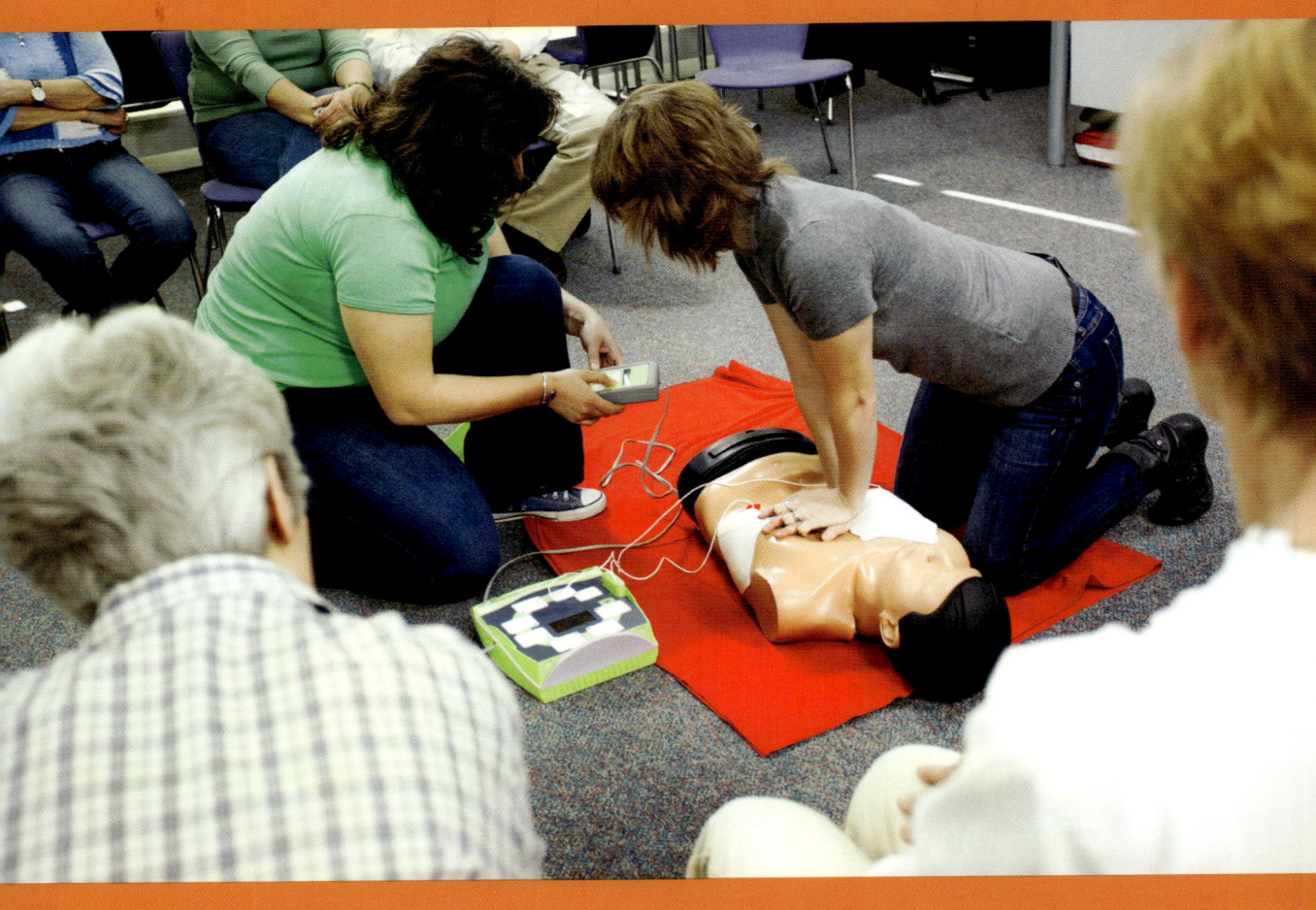
Athletic trainers need to be certified in CPR.

learn first aid and **CPR**. They may work as an assistant to the school's athletic trainer. They might keep the team's first-aid kit well supplied or be responsible for making sure that water is available for the athletes.

Students can also become involved in school sports. Playing and watching sports helps ATs understand the kinds of injuries that can occur. Their firsthand experience helps them teach athletes how to prevent injuries. It also gives them a better understanding of how to treat injuries that do occur.

Anyone who wants to become a **certified** athletic trainer must earn a bachelor's degree in college. More than 70 percent of certified athletic trainers also have a master's degree. There are more than 350 athletic training programs at U.S. colleges. These programs include science classes such as **anatomy**, **biomechanics**, **kinetics**, and **physiology**. Other classes include fitness and exercise, nutrition, budgeting, and record keeping. Practical training classes include how to identify injuries,

To get certified, athletic trainers need to take human anatomy classes.

THINK ABOUT SCIENCE

To become an athletic trainer, a student must take a lot of science courses. Athletic trainers must understand not only how the human body works, but also the best ways to help it heal if injured. The more athletic trainers know about biology and anatomy, the better able they are to help the athlete.

treat injuries, and determine the best **rehabilitation** exercises.

College graduates with a degree in athletic training must take and pass a national certification test. The Board of Certification oversees the certification process. As of 2011, 42 states required certified athletic trainers to become licensed in their state. In some states, athletic trainers have to take a second test to become licensed.

To remain certified, athletic trainers must receive continuing education unit (CEU) credits each year. They can earn them by taking courses at a university. They can also earn them by teaching or attending special classes at conferences. Writing articles for sports medicine journals is another way to earn CEUs.

— CHAPTER 3 —

On the Job

The work athletic trainers do can be very rewarding. They help athletes prepare for their sport before, during, and after an event. Their responsibilities include preventing, identifying, and treating injuries. They also must direct rehabilitation and keep accurate records.

ATs work to prevent injuries from occurring. They show athletes how to stretch, exercise, and condition their muscles and joints before practices or competitions. They also make sure athletes use exercise equipment correctly. ATs encourage the athletes to eat

Athletic trainers help players stretch before games.

healthy foods and to drink plenty of water.

Even with these preventive measures, injuries do happen. When an athlete is hurt, the AT must quickly identify the injury and decide how to treat it. Some ATs can put **splints** and casts on athletes when they get injured. However, all serious injuries are referred to a doctor.

Some of the basic supplies that athletic trainers use are tape, wraps, braces, and splints. These supplies help support weak or sore muscles and joints. They also help

Whatever the injury is, the athletic trainer needs to know how to help.

prevent **sprains** and **strains** from pulled **ligaments** and **tendons**. Cold packs and heat packs help bring down swelling or ease the soreness of a strain or sprain. ATs also use antiseptics to remove germs from wounds, as well as bandages to protect the wounds.

Athletic trainers need to know how to use and operate several kinds of equipment. If someone's neck or spine might be injured, the AT must carefully move the athlete onto a **spine board**. After the injury is treated or healed, a rehabilitation program may be needed for the athlete to

If an athlete is seriously injured, the AT will take him or her off the field for more treatment.

[COOL STEAM CAREERS]

17

Athletic trainers give athletes advice about how to exercise safely.

return to normal health. An athletic trainer assists the athlete in following a program of special activities and exercises that strengthen the recovering muscles or joints.

The **whirlpool** helps athletes with tight or sore arm, leg, and shoulder muscles. Athletic trainers also guide the use of weight machines for warm-up, conditioning, and rehabilitation exercises. New methods of training are constantly being developed.

THINK ABOUT TECHNOLOGY

Up-to-date technology helps athletic trainers do their jobs well. Computer programs help trainers handle their responsibilities accurately and efficiently. They can keep track of schedules as well as their training and rehabilitation programs. Computers are also used for budgets and record keeping. More and more of the equipment that ATs use when working with athletes is also computerized.

— CHAPTER 4 —

Benefits and Disadvantages

If you enjoy sports but are not an athlete, becoming an athletic trainer is a good way to be involved. But like most careers, there are both positive and negative aspects of the job.

As an athletic trainer, you can feel the satisfaction that comes from helping other people. Athletic trainers play an important part in helping keep athletes safe during their sport. They also help make sure athletes are competing at their best physically.

Becoming an athletic trainer can also give you opportunities to work with big-name athletes.

Athletic trainers who work in schools may need to work long hours.

About 800 ATs work with professional athletes on baseball, basketball, football, and hockey teams. Others work with professional golfers, tennis players, race-car drivers, and rodeo competitors.

One disadvantage of being an athletic trainer is that you may have to work long hours. ATs in schools sometimes work 50 to 60 hours a week. They might work six or seven days a week because teams play or practice on weekends. ATs for professional teams might work 12 hours a day during training camps and on practice and game days.

Many trainers use computers and tablets to keep records of their work.

Your schedule may be unpredictable, too. Whether you are working for an individual or a team, you will have to follow the athlete's or team's schedule. This may mean working a lot of nights and weekends. You may have to come in early or stay late to treat injuries or conduct physical therapy sessions. ATs may also be required to travel with the team.

THINK ABOUT MATH

Athletic trainers have to be good at math and managing money. They are responsible for a yearly budget—money that is available for supplies, equipment, and extra staff. They must decide how to spend that money without going over the budget. They must keep accurate records of how much money has been spent and how much is left.

[COOL STEAM CAREERS]

CHAPTER 5

Today and Tomorrow

With more people enjoying physical activity and sports, the need for athletic trainers will continue to grow. The U.S. Bureau of Labor Statistics expects the number of athletic training jobs to increase by 19 percent by 2022. This is faster than the expected growth for other occupations.

About 40 percent of athletic trainers work with sports teams in schools or professional settings. More high schools—and even some elementary and middle schools—are hiring athletic trainers.

More medical clinics and hospitals are adding sports medicine departments. About 34 percent of athletic trainers work in these settings. Doctors observe the ATs' work as they take medical histories, perform parts of physical examinations, and determine basic injuries. ATs in medical clinics also spend time helping patients with rehabilitation.

Since so many people all over the world play sports, the demand for athletic trainers will remain high.

Some athletic trainers work at health clubs or community centers.

About 20 percent of athletic trainers work at YMCAs, gyms, fitness centers, and health clubs. ATs show members how to warm up before exercising and how to use weight-training equipment correctly. They also help members with their rehabilitation exercises. If accidents or injuries occur in these settings, ATs can respond immediately.

Two other work settings for athletic trainers include performing arts centers and the military. Performers can experience the same injuries to their joints and muscles as athletes. Ballet companies, Cirque du Soleil, and the Radio City Music Hall Rockettes have ATs on their staffs. In recent years, some branches of the military service have hired ATs. They treat injuries the recruits suffer, such as sprained ankles and pulled muscles. Because the recruits don't often have time to return for follow-up exams, the ATs give them stretches to practice on their own.

Workers in offices and on assembly lines sometimes

Athletic trainers can help military recruits stay in good shape.

have the same kinds of joint and muscle injuries as athletes. Private companies such as Coca-Cola, FedEx, Frito-Lay, and Nike have hired ATs. They can organize injury prevention programs and manage any injuries that come up. Their efforts can help reduce employee sick leave and companies' health insurance payments.

The yearly salary range differs according to work setting and responsibility. The average salary for athletic trainers in clinics is about $42,000 per year. Athletic trainers in elementary, middle, and high schools earn about $53,000. Those with performing arts companies earn around $54,000. ATs with professional sports teams can earn from $50,000 to $128,000.

A career as an athletic trainer can be exciting and rewarding. There are opportunities to help keep people fit in many different kinds of settings. For sports lovers with a real interest in how the human body works, it might just be a winning career!

THINK ABOUT ART

Athletic trainers are an important part of the performing arts. They work with dancers, musicians, and singers. These ATs create programs to prevent injuries and keep the performers in top condition. With an athletic trainer on-site, not only is the number of injuries reduced, but the operating and production costs are reduced as well.

THINK ABOUT IT

Some athletic trainers compete in sports themselves; others don't. What do you think would be the benefits of an AT working with an athlete who competes in the same sports as him or her? What do you think the challenges would be?

Go online to read more about a famous player suffering an injury— try researching Steve Yzerman getting hit in the eye with a hockey puck, or Kevin Ware breaking his leg during a basketball game. (But don't watch the videos if they will make you feel uncomfortable!) How do you think athletic trainers were able to help them? What were their recoveries like?

Ask your parents or other adults if their workplaces have ever needed athletic trainers on-site. If not, do they think they should hire one in the future? Why or why not? See if you can find a real-life example of an athletic trainer in a non-sports setting.

LEARN MORE

FURTHER READING

Field, Shelly. *Career Opportunities in the Sports Industry*, 3rd ed. New York: Ferguson Publishing, 2004.

Heitzmann, William Ray. *Careers for Sports Nuts and Other Athletic Types*. Chicago: McGraw Hill, 2004.

Reeves, Diane Lindsey, Lindsey Clasen, and Nancy Bond (illustrator). *Career Ideas for Kids Who Like Sports*. New York: Checkmark Books, 2007.

WEB SITES

The Lawrenceville School—Athletic Training Student Aide Program
www.lawrenceville.org/athletics/athletic-training-department/athletic-training-student-aide-program/index.aspx
Learn about one school's Athletic Training Student Aide Program.

National Athletic Trainers' Association
www.nata.org
Find links to NATA's Hall of Fame, professional journal, recent research, and regional and state athletic trainers' associations.

GLOSSARY

anatomy (uh-NAT-uh-mee) the science of how the human body is organized

biomechanics (bye-oh-muh-KAN-iks) the study of how the body's musculoskeletal system works

certified (SUR-tuh-fyed) officially approved to be able to do a job, usually after passing a test

condition (kuhn-DISH-uhn) to get someone into good health

CPR (SEE-PEE-AR) the way to revive someone who has stopped breathing

kinetics (ki-NET-iks) the study of how parts of the body move

ligaments (LIG-uh-muhntz) thick bands of tissue that connect one bone to another bone

physiology (fih-zee-AH-luh-gee) the study of the activities of the body's tissues and cells

rehabilitation (ree-huh-bi-luh-TAY-shuhn) special activities, exercises, or other programs that return an athlete to normal health after an injury

spine board (SPINE BORD) a specially designed board used to prevent an injured person's spine from moving

splints (SPLINTZ) pieces of wood, plastic, or metal used to prevent movement of a joint or to support an injured arm or leg

sprains (SPRAYNZ) stretches or tears of a ligament

strains (STRAYNZ) stretches or tears of a muscle or tendon

tendons (TEN-duhnz) thick bands of tissue that connect a muscle to a bone

whirlpool (WURL-pool) a tub in which jets of air circulate hot or cold water

INDEX

art, 29
athletes, professional, 21
athletic trainers, 6–7
   demand for, 24, 25
   education and training, 8–13
   future of, 24–29
   positive and negatives of the job, 20–23
   salary, 28–29
   supplies and equipment, 15–16
   what they do, 4–7, 14–19
   where they work, 24–28

engineering, 7
equipment and supplies, 15–16
exercise, 6, 13, 18, 19

injuries, 5–6, 7, 14, 15, 27, 29

math, 23

rehabilitation, 13, 14, 25, 27

science, 9, 11, 12
sports, 11

technology, 19, 22